25 Main Street
Newtown, CT 06470

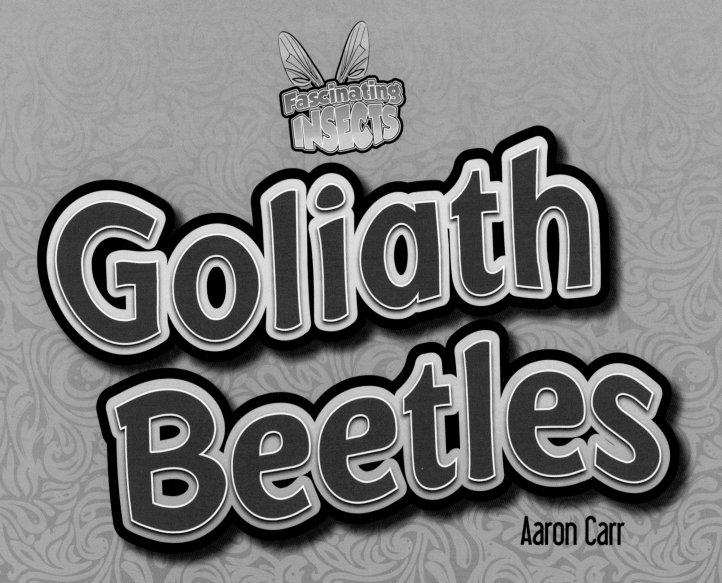

Fascinating INSECTS

Goliath Beetles

Aaron Carr

LET'S READ
AV2
BY WEIGL™
ADDED VALUE • AUDIO VISUAL

www.av2books.com

LET'S READ
AV²
BY WEIGL™
ADDED VALUE • AUDIO VISUAL

Go to **www.av2books.com**, and enter this book's unique code.

BOOK CODE

J670644

AV² by Weigl brings you media enhanced books that support active learning.

AV² provides enriched content that supplements and complements this book. Weigl's AV² books strive to create inspired learning and engage young minds in a total learning experience.

Your AV² Media Enhanced books come alive with...

Audio
Listen to sections of the book read aloud.

Video
Watch informative video clips.

Embedded Weblinks
Gain additional information for research.

Try This!
Complete activities and hands-on experiments.

Key Words
Study vocabulary, and complete a matching word activity.

Quizzes
Test your knowledge.

Slide Show
View images and captions, and prepare a presentation.

... and much, much more!

Published by AV² by Weigl
350 5th Avenue, 59th Floor New York, NY 10118
Website: www.av2books.com   www.weigl.com

Library of Congress Control Number: 2013937272
ISBN 978-1-62127-327-1 (hardcover)
ISBN 978-1-62127-332-5 (softcover)

Printed in the United States of America in North Mankato, Minnesota
1 2 3 4 5 6 7 8 9 0 17 16 15 14 13

052013
WEP040413

Project Coordinator: Aaron Carr   Art Director: Terry Paulhus

Photo Credits
Frantisek Bacovsky: 4, 8, 10, 11, 12, 13, 16, 19; Thomas Winkler: 9; Corbis Images: 14; Getty Images: 3, 6, 20; Alamy: 18.

Goliath Beetles

CONTENTS

3

Meet the goliath beetle.

Goliath beetles are large insects. They are one of the largest insects in the world.

Goliath beetles live in Africa.

In Africa, goliath beetles live in forests.

6

Goliath beetles look like big slugs when they are young.

When they are young, goliath beetles
cover themselves in dirt. They stay
in the dirt while they grow into adults.

Goliath beetles have colorful shells.

Their colorful shells keep them safe.

Goliath beetles have sharp claws.

Their sharp claws
help them climb trees.

Goliath beetles fly
with their large wings.

Their large wings can fold up and hide inside their shells.

Goliath beetles have pointed heads.

Their pointed heads help people tell males from females.

Goliath beetles eat tree sap and fruit.

Eating tree sap and fruit
helps goliath beetles stay healthy.

Goliath beetles also eat dead plants.

By eating dead plants, goliath beetles help keep the forest healthy.

21

GOLIATH BEETLE FACTS

These pages provide more detail about the interesting facts found in the book. They are intended to be used by adults as a learning support to help young readers round out their knowledge of each insect or arachnid featured in the *Fascinating Insects* series.

Pages 4–5

Goliath beetles are large insects. Insects have six jointed legs and bodies with three parts: the head, the abdomen, and the thorax. Insects have hard outer shells called exoskeletons. There are five species of goliath beetles. The largest species, *Goliathus regius*, can reach sizes up to 5.9 inches (15 centimeters) long and 3.9 inches (10 cm) wide. They can weigh more than 3.5 ounces (100 grams), though they only reach this weight in the early stages of life.

Pages 6–7

Goliath beetles live in Africa. Most goliath beetles are found near the equator. They usually make their homes in tropical forests and rainforests. These habitats only have two seasons—the wet season and the dry season. One goliath beetle species has adapted to life in the temperate forests of southern Africa. This is the smallest goliath beetle species. The largest species lives in the African rainforest.

Pages 8–9

Goliath beetles hatch from eggs when they are born. They go through four stages of life: egg, larva, pupa, and adult. The giant, slug-like goliath beetle larvae eat often and grow quickly. The goliath beetle reaches its heaviest weight during the larva stage. The pupa stage begins when the larva burrows underground and wraps itself in a cocoon made of dirt. The goliath beetle transforms into its adult form while in the cocoon. It emerges as a fully grown adult at the start of the wet season.

Pages 10–11

Goliath beetles have colorful shells. The goliath beetle is known for its distinctive coloring. This coloring is primarily made up of stark patches of black and white, though brown is also common. A pair of hard wings, called elytra, make up most of the goliath beetle's colored shell. These wings are not used for flying. Instead, they protect the beetle's body and a second pair of wings that are underneath.

Pages 12–13

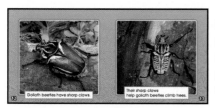

Goliath beetles have sharp claws. Each of the goliath beetle's six legs ends in a pair of claws. These claws are called tarsi. The tarsi are very strong and help the goliath beetle grip trees and other large plants. This allows the goliath beetle to climb in search of food. Adult goliath beetles spend most of their time climbing in trees.

Pages 14–15

Goliath beetles fly with their large wings. The goliath beetle has larger wings than a sparrow. Goliath beetles keep these wings folded under the elytra when not in use. When the beetle flies, the wings unfold and spread up to 8 inches (20 cm) wide from one wing tip to the other. The wings are flexible and usually black in color.

Pages 16–17

Goliath beetles have pointed heads. Male and female goliath beetles have different head shapes. Females have a wedge-shaped head. The female uses her wedge-shaped head to dig holes in the ground. The holes are used for laying eggs. Males, on the other hand, have horned heads. The Y-shaped horns are used to fight other males for territory and for mating purposes.

Pages 18–19

Goliath beetles eat tree sap and fruit. They will eat a variety of plants found in their natural environment. However, they prefer sugary foods such as tree sap and fruit. In the larva stage of development, goliath beetles need much more protein in their diet than other kinds of beetles. People who raise goliath beetles sometimes feed the larvae high-protein cat or dog food.

Pages 20–21

Goliath beetles break down dead plants. The goliath beetle plays an important role in its ecosystem. Goliath beetles are decomposers. This means they eat dead and decaying plants and fruits. The goliath beetle's body digests its food and produces nutrient-rich waste. This helps return nutrients to the soil, which in turn helps plants grow and keeps the ecosystem healthy.

KEY WORDS

Research has shown that as much as 65 percent of all written material published in English is made up of 300 words. These 300 words cannot be taught using pictures or learned by sounding them out. They must be recognized by sight. This book contains 35 common sight words to help young readers improve their reading fluency and comprehension. This book also teaches young readers several important content words. These words are paired with pictures to aid in learning and improve understanding.

Page	Sight Words First Appearance	Page	Content Words First Appearance
4	the	4	goliath beetle
5	are, in, large, of, one, they, world	5	insects
6	live	6	Africa, forests
8	big, like, look, when, young	8	slugs
9	grow, into, while	9	adults, dirt
10	have	10	shells
11	keep, their, them	12	claws
13	help, trees	14	wings
14	with	16	females, males
15	and, can, up	18	fruit, sap
16	from, heads, people, tell		
18	eat		
20	also, by, plants		

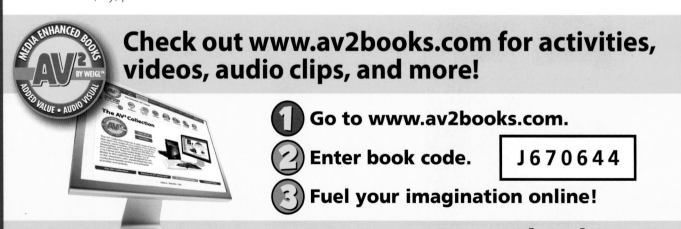

Check out www.av2books.com for activities, videos, audio clips, and more!

1 Go to www.av2books.com.

2 Enter book code. | J 6 7 0 6 4 4 |

3 Fuel your imagination online!

www.av2books.com